I0468197

Get Them To Say Yes

For Business & Job Interviews

By

David K. Ewen, M.Ed.

ISBN-13: 978-1530142071

ISBN-10: 1530142075

Copyright © 2016, Ewen Prime Company

Get Them To Say Yes

For Business & Job Interviews

By
David K. Ewen, M.Ed.

A Production of:

Forest Academy
&
Your World Discovered

Two part book

The book "Get Them To Say Yes" comes in two parts. The first part is the presentation of content and material relevant two job interviews and negotiations. The second part is a workbook for homework practice. The workbook offers three opportunities to practice for the purpose of seeing successful progression. This serves as a confirmation of learning to build confidence and satisfaction. The goal is to head in the direction of success. Included in the content of this book are other resources that can be used to go beyond the scope of this book. Look for them and take advantage of them.

Get Them To Say Yes

For Business & Job Interviews

By
David K. Ewen, M.Ed.

Thank you

I don't know who originally said the quote "behind a successful man is a great woman" or something like that. I know that it is true because my wife Maria has helped make me become who I am today. Without her support and patience the success of developing this content in material over the duration of more than 11 years on tour would not be possible. Many times she would travel with me to different colleges, universities, and other educational institutions in the 7 states of New York and New England. She has been by my side through all of it. When Maria sees the cover of this book, she sees 11 years, 25000 miles in traveling, thousands of audience members, and the countless hours to put into curriculum development. She has been through the highs and the lows of a speaking tour and knows the true hard effort that goes into making success. I thank my wife Maria for being with me during this journey so that I would not be alone. We both know the value of hard work and perseverance. I was never alone in this journey. God watched both of us and protected us during this venture. With that, I give a heartfelt thank you.

Get Them To Say Yes

For Business & Job Interviews

By
David K. Ewen, M.Ed.

A Production of:

Forest Academy
&
Your World Discovered

Have you ever wondered how some people can close deals or easily get hired at a job? Those people have practiced successful methodologies necessary to achieve success. The content and material shared in this presentation have been researched, tested, and put into practice with proven results. The tips, tricks, and techniques are applicable to a variety of situations and industries. If given the secrets then we are empowered to achieve success. After all, isn't that what all of us want to do? You are empowered and you can. Learn how.

Gift

This content and material are presented in a variety of forms. On occasion I provide to formats available to the general public for free. It gives me great satisfaction when I see a young person get their first job or a seasoned adult reach their career goals. As a public speaker and talk show host, I enjoy the heartfelt enthusiasm of success seen on the faces of my audience members. Every person should donate their experience and knowledge to sow the seed of something greater. I believe it is a responsibility that we as a shared community have with each other. I take on this responsibility by providing the ebook for this content free during a five day period twice per year and occasionally hosting a free online workshop seminar open to the public. In addition, this content is available online in many formats at a very low cost.

Preface
Purpose
Foundation

This content and material begin in some way as a memoir in appreciation to those who have helped plant the seeds that supported the development of the paperback book, e-book, album, video book, and online lecture. As a professor I usually start my lectures by explaining a little about my background so that students understand and recognize the meaning and revelation behind what I am saying. It is important for students to recognize that what is being presented is based on factual hands-on experience and not opinion and hearsay.

This is being shared with you so that you know who the author is and recognize the value of what is being presented.

From the Author

When I impart knowledge to an audience, I make it clear that I have made all of the mistakes such as trusting the wrong people and making the wrong investments. I've done it all. However I've made the corrections to leave the errors behind and follow the success ahead. The mistakes I have made in business are the common one everyone makes without experience. They are based on wrong assumptions. My lectures often talk about the wrong way to do something and why it is wrong based on experience. Then I talk about the right way to do something based on the experience of success and leaving the failures behind.

I owe a lot to the organizations that I have founded which have served as vehicles of exploration. During this exploration, I have met many amazing people who I respect and admire who have put tracks in front of me to leave me alone mentored success. My obedience to this guidance has prevented my efforts from falling off the cliff into disaster. I am so grateful and thankful. This is what I want to share. I begin by giving great thanks to those who have come across my path with the organizations that I have found it. They are:

- Ewen Prime Company
- New England Publishers Assoc.
- Boston Voyager
- forest Academy
- Kelvin Projects
- EPN News
- The EPN Enterprise

Hands-On

The source of content and material come from a variety of lectures and presentations given over the years. I remember speaking at the Connecticut authors Association with about 50 attendees talking about publicity and marketing to help others better represent themselves in the book selling market place. There was another time when I held a lecture in New London Connecticut width 75 attendees about job interviewing and presentation skills. That was followed by an email received explaining an attendee got a job. As the director of the New England Publishers Association I conducted a year-long tour in 1998 at New England bookstores to teach writers and authors how to represent themselves in the marketplace as leaders in book publishing.

Internationally, I work with individuals in the Middle East, China, and Japan how to be better business leaders. AT 52 locations in the seven states of New York and New England for 11 years I toured the region lecturing on entrepreneurial studies and leadership in the marketplace. The audience question have been turned through research and apply to factual hands-on experience. Understand that this content and material is based fully on factual hands-on experience.

- David K. Ewen, M.Ed.

Dedication

I dedicate this material and content to all the people I have helped succeed in business deals, freelancing opportunities, and job interviews. These specially recognized people are from Japan, the UK, China, Australia, Canada, the Middle East, India, and the United States. Beginning first in the seven states of New York and New England, followed by countries around the world, the success my students have demonstrated gives me heartfelt appreciation for their trust in the objectives of this material and the obedience to follow the guidelines which in turn resulted in their success. For that I am grateful. Without their success this book, album, movie, and online lecture would not be possible. Thank you. - David K. Ewen, M.Ed.

Appreciation

I give appreciation to the members of the **New England Publishers Association** originally founded in 1998. After being sold and later transformed, many of the members remained. This initiative and foundation effort taught me the lessons of organizational theory and behavior in business relationships. This includes everything from business deals to freelancing, to job interviews. I owe much to the original members of the New England Publishers Association. I am proud to have founded this organization so long ago and have seen the subsequent fruits of success flourish throughout the New England community today.

- David K. Ewen, M.Ed.

I would also like to give appreciation to my students at colleges and universities where I have taught all over New York and New England during an 11 year tour called **"The Professor Lecture Series"** from **Forest Academy**. They have made me better with business strategies by asking challenging questions which positioned me into researching the right answers that are now found in the multiple books that I have joyfully published. Each student brought their style of eagerness to learn which talk me how to discern people's needs and how to satisfy their thirst for knowledge. The diversity on college campuses and university lecture halls has given me the opportunity to understand people in a discerning manner so that I could be better at presenting knowledge beneficial to others.

- David K. Ewen, M.Ed.

INTRO

This material is designed to help individuals with reaching future goals associated with business deals, freelancing opportunities, and getting hired at a job. It serves as a communication resource that enables empowerment for people to succeed in reaching agreements and winning opportunities. The material has cumulated since 1994 when I first launched **Ewen Prime Company** as a publishing house. Later in 1998, when I founded the **New England Publishers Association** with a membership of over 300, a higher dimension of understanding people and business was cumulated. During the 11 years beginning in 2004 as a university lecturer in the seven states of New York and New England, the theories and methodologies that had been cumulated we're fully tested.

As a touring professor at **Forest Academy** in the seven states of New York and New England for 11 years, I hosted "**The Professor Lecture Series**" in many lecture halls and classrooms. During this travel, I worked with many business leaders and students of entrepreneurial studies. I appreciate their challenging questions that forced me to know the right answers to give them success.

After each session, attendees and visitors would write an evaluation to be delivered to the institution. These evaluations kept bringing me back to 52 venues for 11 years in New York and New England.

The free sharing of knowledge at liberty has been scattered with over 50 books published, several movies, albums, and radio shows. My appreciation go to all who attended, visited, and shared to make the **Professor Lecture Series** at **Forest Academy** a success.

More recently beginning in the year 2014, the tested theories and methodologies were put into practice around the world in Japan, Turkey, China, the UK, Australia, India, Canada, in the United States. This **educational ambassador work** supports enrichment and unity within our global community. This comes from the **EPN Enterprise** established in August 1015. By 2016, this material and content accumulated a collection of over 21 years of solid industry experience working directly with business leaders, famous celebrities, broadcast media, universities, and community leaders. Everything contained herein has been researched, tested, and put into practice. Students have reported back successful results and have attributed this content in material to reaching their goals.

When I earned my masters degree in education in 1988 (M.Ed.) at **Cambridge College** in Cambridge, Massachusetts, I had published a paper that theorized three teaching methodologies that when combined are effective for the learning process. Some people learn by listening. Others learn by demonstration. Others learn by physical action. All people learn by combining listening, demonstration, and physical action together. The research, testing, and putting into practice this material has been presented to colleges and universities in New York and New England using all three teaching methods.

- David K. Ewen, M.Ed.

Questions

There are a series of questions that an interviewer asks an interviewee to understand the following:

- Ability of candidate
- Willingness of candidate

The ability is the skill. The willingness is the commitment.

The skills are in the form of

- Hard skills from training
- Soft skills from experience

The job of the interviewer is to understand and verify the ability and willingness of a candidate to take on and assigned venture. The job of the candidate is to demonstrate by way of answering questions the ability and willingness that they have to take on an venture. The ability is a representation of skills that were learned through education or experience. There are two kinds of skills. One is the hard skills that are developed through training and education. The other or soft skills associated with behavioral responses that are developed through experience.

The willingness is represented in such a way that a sense of commitment is demonstrated. Proving a willingness to accept long-term responsibility in the form of commitment is challenging because only answers to questions can be used during an interview. The words have to be chosen carefully so that the interviewer can discern that the willingness of the candidate is real. One way this feels is Candidate tries to oversell them self rather than speak in a matter-of-fact sort of way with facts.

The kind of **interviewers** who ask interviewees (candidates) questions include general topics shown below.

- Managers seeking to hire staff
- Businesses shopping for vendors
- Business Partnership Development

The interviewee is among a collection of candidates that the interviewer considers.

A special set of questions that the interviewer asks are designed to:

- Interrogate to Understand
- Investigate Mysteries
- Discover Meaning
- Find Facts
- Negotiate
- Make Deals
- Discern Behavior
- Reveal Truth

The kind of **interviewees**, who serve as candidates, are competing to win the acceptance of the interviewers. Some examples are:

- People seeking to be hired for a job
- Vendors prospecting clients
- Potential business partners
- Fundraising organizations
- Grant writers seeking funds
- Workplace colleague collaboration

Interviewees are candidates who answer questions from the interviewer.

They must appeal to the desires of the interviewer to garnish acceptance. They do this by showing the benefits of their features founded by hard skills and soft skills.

- Hard skills – Trained learning
- Soft skills – Behavioral experience

The goal of the interviewer is to select the best interviewee from a collection of candidates.

The goal of the interviewee is to be considered the best selection from the population of candidates being considered.

The goal of both the interviewer and interviewee is to collaborate with synergy to reach common goals in a way that reaches expectations of both parties.

On occasion, a probationary period is agreed upon to determine if the synergy intended by both parties holds true for the long term. This serves as a trial period that measures the level of synergy that identifies compatibility of the recently formed relationship.

In this presentation, a set of questions and answers identifies common investigative measures to determine compatibility between and interviewer and candidate (interviewee).

The questions and answers shared in this presentation have taught in lectures in different parts of Asia, the Middle East, and America. The compiled list of investigative questions are common worldwide.

In the discussion found in this material, a few examples will be given that can be custom tailored to a variety of situations. The goal is to impart the revelation of the meaning of questions so that candidates can offer the best answer.

The round table is an expression where an interviewer and candidate get together to share common knowledge and experiences to learn from each other.   Each side investigates each other to determine level of compatibility to see if synergy exists.

Interviewers have a choice among candidates while candidates being interviewed are seeking the acceptance of the interviewer.   The candidate knows that eh interviewer has the choice to accept or decline a partnership or collaboration.

The choice that the candidate has in the event of being declined is to move on to the next available interviewer. Candidates prepare for being rejected as a worse case scenario. Interviewers are prepared to make a choice and to offer acceptance or rejection.

The questions of negotiation, interviewing, and surveying are so numerous to cover here, but the questions presented cover all major categories. They serve as the most important foundation. The completion of this material will give understanding of how interviewers and candidates talk around the world. Those who fill the candidates role will know how best to present answers to position themselves in positive light toward acceptance. After all, that is the goal.

For interviewers, this material will help build skill toward discernment to recognize the best candidates.

A "win-win" situation is when an interviewer selects the best candidate and the candidate is chosen among all other possibilities. The goal of the candidate is to be more than a possibility.

Model Example

In any negotiation or interview, the best model to understand how questions and answers go back and forth is the job interview. This model is reflective of what happens in business deals such as a contractor looking for new client or vendors looking for new companies to represent. In any interrogative discussion, there is the interviewer who asks questions and a candidate who is prospecting for an opportunity to be accepted. Candidates are aware that they are not alone within a pool of opportunity of candidates that an interviewer can select from. The questions that are asked and answered are designed to discern the worthiness of long-term collaboration. In some cases the collaboration maybe short terms such as in freelancing opportunities.

The mindset the candidates must have is that of confidence and a discerning awareness of what the interviewer considers worthy. This requires an open intuitive mind with an alert way of thinking. Although this is difficult to do, practicing a set of fixed questions can help with the preparation. The common application discussed in this material will be the job interview however it will be worded in a way to satisfy multiple applications. This includes business deals and winning over freelancing opportunities.   Many   candidates discover difficulty in   representing themselves. This material will help.

Questions

The questions of negotiation, interviewing, and surveying are so numerous to cover here, but the questions presented cover all major categories. The completion of this material will give understanding of how interviewers and candidates talk around the world. Those who fill the candidates role will know how best to present answers to position themselves in positive light toward acceptance. After all, that is the goal.

For interviewers, this material will help build skill toward discernment to recognize the best candidates.

A "win-win" situation is when an interviewer selects the best candidate and the candidate is chosen among all other possibilities. The goal of the candidate is to be more than a possibility.

Body Language

Many people do not know that body language plays a role in communication. Having hands clasped in front of you shows that you have a fence in front of you indicating that something is hidden. By leaving the hand separated and showing the palms shows that you have freedom of information with nothing to hide. That is a more welcoming posture. Instead, occupy your hands with a small notepad and a pen to take notes. The note taking process demonstrates that what you are being told has value. It shows interest in the conversation. The benefit of note taking is a prevent you from leaning backwards which is a sign of disinterest. By writing notes on a pad at a table positions the body to be sitting upright and slightly leaning forward demonstrating interest in the conversation.

The motion of the head is important in communication. By nodding in the affirmative shows agreement and acceptance of what is being presented. This shows a willingness toward collaboration and the ability to be obedient construction. Addition to the head nods, it is important in to maintain eye contact to demonstrate focused attention with no distraction. This behavior and body language proves that you have recognized purpose and value in the conversation.

The note taking with eye contact and the occasional head nod will go a long way toward successful negotiation. Incidentally, this body language helps to reduce stress and increase focused attention. This serves as a win-win situation for both the interviewer and the Candidate.

Identity

The first question we will discuss is related to identity. Usually that question involves stating who you are or the question of tell me about yourself. This explains why you are part of the negotiation process. An example is if you are applying for a job the question may be asked why you applied.

Everyone has a long lengthy history and it makes no sense to go into detail that would not be relevant to the conversation. The negotiation is at the interview table so it is best to explain why you are there. Explain the purpose of what brought you to the interview table. This will give the answer to explain the identity of your representation and who you are . It is necessary to be brief and to the point. If additional information is necessary, the interviewer will ask more questions.

The benefit of the additional questions if you will know what the interviewer wants to learn from you.

When the question is asked *"Why you are here?"* or what brings you here, it is best to answer the brief history of what brought you to the table. That type of question makes sense and the purpose is clear. A question such as *"Tell me about yourself?"* is very much open ended but still holds the same meaning as *"What brought you to the interview table?"*. Remember that the question tell me about yourself does not mean to provide a biography and a lengthy history. The answer intended is relevant to how the interview took place and the reason behind it. Any further questions will help guide the rest of the conversation in a less vague way.

Performance

One of the ways an interviewer will ask a candidate to describe their ability to handle stress is to simply ask the question relating to describing a stressful situation. If the answer does describe a stressful situation, that means that there is a threshold of stress in which case the candidate identifies the situation as stressful. The better answer is to not show that threshold interesting hey from identifying a stressful situation. The best answer is to indicate that you do not experience stress. It is better to say that some days are busier than others where challenges may arise. A good answer would be followed by indicating that you handle stress by being a problem solver and not worrying about the problem.

The dangers of the question relating to stress has to do with exposing an inability to handle stress. The best way to protect against that type of exposure is to not acknowledge the recognition of stress, rather to demonstrate the ability to handle challenging situations. The challenging situations should not be identified as stress, but rather as opportunities for problem solving. This type of question asked by a interviewer can prove to be valuable if the candidate is able to demonstrate that they are a problem solver able to handle challenges because situations are not identified as stress.

Hard Skills

There are two types of skills that people have and share them as a candidate when talking to interviewers. One of them is hard skills and the other one is soft skills. The hard skills are identified are the technical skills developed through training and education. The soft skills are related to the human element of behavior that cannot be practiced and rehearsed. They are developed through time by handling situations. The hard skills are proven buy diploma and certifications. They are authenticated by experience that is verifiable.

When preparing for an interview, only the hard skills can be prepared by having ready information on practical hands-on experience that followed training and education. The soft skills are demonstrated and authenticated during the interview process.

Desire

Interviewers look to find the desire of the candidate. They will ask questions such as why are you here or why did you apply for the position. The answer must be in the form of the positives indicating interest, desire, and a feeling of want. The answer must also show a demonstration of confidence in ability through testimonial experience of achievement and success. The best way to prepare for this type of question is to have ready relevant testimonial experiences of achievement and success. It is common for to feel good about themselves and speak more energetically when they talk about their successes when it relates to why they are being interviewed in the first place.

Strengths

What is felt to be the easiest question to answer is related to what are your strengths. The mistake people make is they talk about strength that most other people have. Of course most people will say that they are hardworking. If you say the same then you will blend in with all the other candidates and not stand out. The answer should indicate accolades and distinctions that separates you from other candidates. The strength that the interviewer is looking for is the uniqueness you have that separates you from others and places you above others. When thinking of the best accolades and distinctions to share consider what would be best to mention that would be memorable.

Weakness

A challenging question to ask and share in an interview is related to your weaknesses. The important thing is not to look like you have something to hide when asked this type of question. It is true that every person has a weakness and so there is no hiding it. The best way to answer this question is to not explain a current weakness that has not been overcome. It is much better to explain a former weakness and to conclude the discussion by explaining clearly how you overcame the weakness. If a follow up question relates to any additional weaknesses, then answer the question in the same way by explaining former weaknesses that have been overcome. Always explain how the weakness has been overcome and eliminated. This demonstrates problem solving abilities.

Future Plans

The calm and quiet associated with questions relating to plans are separated by future short term plans and future long term plans. Both questions relate to identifying your vision, mission, and goal. Your vision is what you see yourself to be in the future. The mission is how you will accomplish that. The goal identifies when that mission is complete and the vision is satisfied. The distinction between short term goals and long term goals is related to professional and personal goals. Professional goals can be changed by external influences. Personal goals have more control by the individual. Short term goals are job related or business related. Long term goals can be related to short term goals, but are more specific to personal and life goals.

When answering questions related to short term goals it is important that the conversation be specific to the evolution of progress that goes beyond the purpose of the interview. For example the discussion related to a job interview would include working towards a promotion. The discussion of long term goal is more specific to career goals or business that have personal meaning for accomplishment. The long term goals are a person's definition of the apex of their success either in business or career.

Short Term

When asked questions relating to short term goals, a person is best prepared by knowing what the next step beyond the current agreement being discussed. By knowing this next step and discussing it paves the way toward a demonstration of commitment. This shows that the current level agreement being discussed will not result in boredom or disinterest. It demonstrates the importance of a foundation necessary to reach the next step. When talking about short term goals, it is necessary to be fully aware of the progression of expansion and next steps to migrate beyond what is being discussed and agreed upon at the interview table. This shows planning and forethought. Interviewers want to see this from a candidate.

Long Term

The difference between short term goals and long term goals is that short term goals focus on commitment to an agreement and long term goals use short-term goals to satisfy personal commitments. For example short term goals reflect what an individual may do for a company if they are higher. An example is working toward a promotion. Long term goals are career oriented that reflect a pass over many years that is consistent and satisfy personal desires. A candidate who indicates limited goals demonstrates limited success plans. A candidate who has struggles demonstrates high expectations. This demonstrates a level of ambition.

Short term goals indicates a measurement of commitment. Long term goals indicates a measurement of ambition. When an interviewer asks questions about short term and long term goals, they are seeking an understanding to the candidates commitment and ambition. Commitment relates to short term goals. Ambition relates to long-term goals. Candidates with good answers relating to these types of questions are able to articulate their level of commitment and ambition. Commitment is better described with more immediate short term planning. Ambition is represented by a long term forecast in plans.

Consideration

When the question is asked why a candidate should be considered, this is an opportunity for the candidate to talk about accolades and distinctions that separate them from other candidates. The mistake many candidates make is they explained that they are of higher value and work harder than other candidates. That type of answer is so cliché and common. The cliché answer should be avoided. The question being asked in reference to why a candidate should be considered is related to a uniqueness that is defined by accolades and distinctions that are not recognized by most other candidates. This type of answer is one of the hardest to prepare if there is no unique accolade or distinctions to discuss.

An example of accolades and distinctions can include being published or receiving an award. Some forgotten examples of accolades and distinctions are the valuable volunteer efforts that demonstrate commitment. Very often volunteer efforts result in unique behavior that requires time management and commitment to an organization's vision and mission. Volunteer efforts are done by choice and discussing them as an accolade or distinction demonstrates a willingness to participate in a worthy cause. Most often volunteer efforts result in leadership roles which is a skill set appropriately represented as a candidates accolade and distinction that is unique from other candidates.

Questions !

During a time of questioning, a candidate maybe ask if they have any questions. The mistake some candidates make is that they say no questions are to be asked. The error in judgement comes from an effort to end the interview quickly into incorrectly think of it as good time management. That is not the purpose of an interviewer to ask a candidate if they have questions. A candidate should ask questions that are specific enough in such a way that it proves they fully understand the other party or the organization that the interviewer represents. This shows interest and demonstrates that the candidate knows why they are in a negotiating process. A candidate must prepare in advance some example questions to ask in such a situation.

Job Interview

There are a certain set of questions that are standard for job interviews. Although they may be standardized, they may be asked in different ways to be industry specific and job application specific. The questions following represent the most common type of investigative interview questions for candidates for jobs and cliental. This also applies to candidates looking for new clients in business partnerships and unified ventures in global enterprises. The questions that are asked must be answered in a way to demonstrate relevancy and a positive representation. The common set of questions follows.

Questions & Answers

1. Tell me about yourself
2. Describe a stressful situation.
3. Hard Skill Questions (industry related)
4. Why did you apply for this position?
5. What is your greatest strength?
6. Why do you want to work for Turkish Airlines?
7. What are your short term plans?
8. What are your long term plans?
9. Why should I hire you for this position?
10. Do you have questions for us?

These are the questions to be practiced, rehearsed, and memorized.

Next Steps

A lot of things have been presented in this content and material. For successful results, it is important to rehearse by putting this material into practice. This involves two or more people working together to conduct a role play that mimics a real situation. The goal is to act as a real life scenario that simulates what would most likely happen in a business deal or job interview. As the practice continues, changes are made so that a personal style of responding to questions is effectively developed. Knowing how to answer a question is not the same as being able to put skills into practice. It must be rehearsed and practiced time and time again. One of the best ways to learn is by doing and acting out the action. This develops experience. Do not make the mistake of avoiding practicing. The effort is necessary. Attempting shortcuts results in failure and frustration.

Practice

1. Tell me about yourself.
2. Describe a stressful situation.
3. Hard Skill Questions (Industry related)
4. Why did you apply for this position?
5. What is your greatest strength?
6. Why do you want to work for this job?
7. What are your short term plans?
8. What are your long term plans?
9. Why should I hire you for this position?
10. Do you have questions for us?

These are the questions to be practiced, rehearsed, and memorized.

Learn More

This is my second book related to job hunting and interview skills. My first book is titled Employment Success With A New Job. It is found on Amazon.

Employment Success With A New Job
ISBN-10: 1497508878
ISBN-13: 978-1497508873
Available as paperback & e-book

The content was presented at a conference for the first time in a packed room of job seekers in New London, Connecticut. The initial results of the conference was an audience member. had an interview and was hired at a job within 24 hours. Additional success stories followed.

Following that success, it made sense to share more information by writing "Get Them To Say Yes".

- David K. Ewen, M.Ed.

Entrepreneurs and Business Leaders

As a professor of Entrepreneurial Studies, I have lectured the seven states of New York and New England talking with business leaders on how to be successful in their ventures. The book below is one of many books published as a result of my lectures. I choose this one as a guide for entrepreneurs to understand how best to represent themselves in the marketplace. It is available in both paperback and e-book on Amazon

Publicity Made Simple
ISBN-10: 1461122627
ISBN-13: 978-1461122623

The content of the book publicity made simple has been used in many different lectures that apply to entrepreneurs, business leaders, consultants, advisors, authors, artists, musicians, filmmakers, politicians, lawyers, accountants, store owners, and public speakers.

- David Ewen

Conclusion

In conclusion, people can achieve success in business deals and job interviews if they put into practice what is learned here in this set of content and materials. Absorbing the knowledge is not enough. It is absolutely critical that the rehearsal and the practicing generates the experience to achieve success. It is important to note that the methodologies discussed are proven through research and testing and demonstrated by being put into practice.

To success !

David K. Ewen, M.Ed.

Workbook

The next part of this book is the homework practice. It is the workbook where you can apply what you have learned and put new knowledge into practice. It is included as part of the entire book so that you can refer to what you have already read. It is important to respond to answers not by emotion and opinion. Please avoid emotion and opinion. Focus more on why the interviewer would be asking the question and what the meaning behind that question is. Think about the purpose of the interviewer's question and what value it has for them. Stick with facts and relevancy to the question and also relevancy to the purpose of the question. Refer to this book for guidance when in doubt.

Workbook

Homework Practice

First (1) Practice

Tell me about yourself

Describe a stressful situation.

(Hard Skill Questions)
Industry specific

Why did you apply for this position?

What is your greatest strength?

Why do you want to work for this company at job location?

What are your short term plans?

What are your long term plans?

Why should I hire you for this position?

Do you have questions for us?

Workbook

Second (2)
Practice

Tell me about yourself

Describe a stressful situation.

(Hard Skill Questions)
Industry specific

Why did you apply for this position?

What is your greatest strength?

Why do you want to work for this company at job location?

What are your short term plans?

What are your long term plans?

Why should I hire you for this position?

Do you have questions for us?

www.ingramcontent.com/pod-product-compliance
Lightning Source LLC
Chambersburg PA
CBHW060353190526
45169CB00002B/581